High School Math the Easy Way

Simple Strategies for Homeschool Parents in Over Their Heads

Lee Binz,
The HomeScholar

© 2015 by **The HomeScholar LLC**

All Rights Reserved. No part of this publication may be reproduced in any form or by any means, including scanning, photocopying, or otherwise without prior written permission of the copyright holder.

First Printing, 2015

Printed in the United States of America

ISBN: 1511805374
ISBN-13: 978-1511805377

Disclaimer: Parents assume full responsibility for the education of their children in accordance with state law. College requirements vary, so make sure to check with the colleges about specific requirements for homeschoolers. We offer no guarantees, written or implied, that the use of our products and services will result in college admissions or scholarship awards.

High School Math the Easy Way

Simple Strategies for Homeschool Parents in Over Their Heads

What are "Coffee Break Books"?

High School Math The Easy Way is part of The HomeScholar's Coffee Break Book series.

Designed especially for parents who don't want to spend hours and hours reading a 400-page book on homeschooling high school, each book combines Lee's practical and friendly approach with detailed, but easy-to-digest information, perfect to read over a cup of coffee at your favorite coffee shop!

Never overwhelming, always accessible and manageable, each book in the series will give parents the tools they need to tackle the tasks of homeschooling high school, one warm sip at a time.

Everything about these Coffee Break Books is designed to suggest simplicity, ease and comfort - from the size (fits in a purse), to the font and paragraph length (easy on the eyes), to the price (the same as a Starbucks Venti Triple Caramel Macchiato). Unlike a fancy coffee drink, however, these books are guilt-free pleasures you will want to enjoy again and again!

Table of Contents

What are "Coffee Break Books"? v
Embracing the Suck 9
Correct Sequence 13
Correct Curriculum 17
Correct Attitude 21
Correct Speed 25
Curriculum Options 31
Games and Supplements......................................39
Nine Ways to Actually Get Math Done This Year..47
Math Records...61
The Home Stretch 65
The HomeScholar Answers Parent Questions.......69
Homeschooling Geeks..83
Who is Lee Binz and What Can She Do for Me?..97
Testimonials 99
Also From The HomeScholar... 101

Introduction

Embracing the Suck

Of all the subjects I hear homeschoolers moan about, math is at the top of the list! It seems like such hard work and can be overwhelming, especially when you reach high school. It takes a lot of time, practice, and review. It's a lot like washing your hair: lather, rinse, and repeat. It's something your child needs to do every day or close to every day.

Everybody has different feelings about math. I was always confident with it because I had a lot of math training. Just between you and me, I did fail Calculus in college, getting a 0.7 my first time through. After I met my husband, I received a 3.7 because he tutored me. Thanks again, sweetie!

Even for math-loving parents it can be challenging. As my children got older, I got to the point where I had no idea what was going on in math. I had been confident teaching through Algebra 1 and Geometry classes. About half way through Algebra 2, though, I was completely befuddled. At that point I joined the ranks of "in over my head" homeschool parents! Almost every parent will get to the point where they don't know what they're doing in math, feeling incompetent and stressed, and like they don't know how to teach it.

Some parents have a teaching degree in high school math and feel confident, but those parents are few and far-between. In my experience, many parents do not remember Algebra 1 class, or they never even got as far as Algebra 1 in high school. These parents tend to freak out in the very early stages of math.

The other extreme are parents who are scientists or engineers and took tons of math in college, but can't remember anything from their earlier Algebra 1 or

Geometry classes. In my experience, almost everybody loses it at some point while teaching math. Eventually, we all throw up our hands in despair and feel like giving up.

Feelings of insecurity and anxiety are universal. I will teach you strategies that can make you confident, self-assured, and give you a plan for what you need to do and how to get there from here. Math can seem like a hassle at times, but we can still ensure it gets done. The real value of math is teaching kids to work hard and instill the value of hard work. It's not easy and it takes a lot of effort. But nothing teaches children to work hard quite as effectively as high school math. If math is not your forte, don't be afraid; there are many things you can do to make it as painless as possible, both for you and your children.

You can do this. Don't give up!

Lee Binz, The HomeScholar

Chapter 1

Correct Sequence

In what order do you need to teach math? It may surprise you that the order of math covered doesn't matter as much as ensuring math is taught for four full years in high school. Your child's high school transcript needs to include four or more credits of math. Four years of math is important because it's required for high school graduation in every state. It's also important because almost all colleges require a full four years of math.

Even if your child already has four or five years of math by the time they start high school, you still want to teach four years of math while they're in high school (at high school age). However, that doesn't mean your child has to do four years of upper level math, including calculus. It just means they should continue to work at their own level and keep moving forward every year.

Yes, it's wonderful to cover calculus in high school, but not everyone is going to get there. Just because they don't get to calculus doesn't mean they can't get into college! Cover math every single year regardless of the level they achieve.

The sequence may vary. There are two ways math is usually introduced:

- Algebra 1 – Geometry – Algebra 2 – Trigonometry or Pre-Calculus – Calculus

OR

- Algebra 1 – Algebra 2 – Geometry – Trigonometry or Pre-Calculus – Calculus.

Try to have Geometry class completed before eleventh grade if you can. Children take the PSAT, SAT, or the ACT in eleventh grade and those tests include geometry. If Geometry class is finished before eleventh grade, your child will score better on these tests. For that reason, I prefer the first sequence option because they're more likely to complete Geometry class before eleventh grade.

Geometry is completely different from algebra, much like biology is different than chemistry. Kids that hate algebra may love geometry. Introducing geometry in the middle gives kids a break. Geometry class also has some review of Algebra 1 concepts in it. As they balance numbers, they use some of the skills learned in Algebra 1. By completing Algebra 1 followed by Geometry class, your child gets a whole year of Algebra 1 practice before going on to Algebra 2. It can help students who are not secure in their Algebra 1 skills get those skills into their brains before they have to start Algebra 2.

Chapter 2

Correct Curriculum

We all have our preferences, but in the end, there isn't one "best" curriculum for everyone, despite what sales people may tell you at homeschool conventions. There's no magic program that will guarantee your child will love math, but there is one key which will at least prevent them from HATING it, and that is to use a curriculum that fits your child. It has a lot to do with personal preference.

Get some feedback on your curriculum from your teen. Present them with several different options, and let them choose the one they prefer. You might be surprised by their choices. When I homeschooled, I was completely shocked at my son's choice of Saxon for math. I had previously rejected that option. Personally, I hated the look of it - all print and no pictures - but that's exactly why my son loved it! He likes numbers and thought pictures just got in the way. Imagine what would have happened if I had brought home a curriculum that I liked, based on my preferences, with many photos and different colors! He would have hated it, and might have ended up hating math, thinking it just wasn't for him.

Choose a well-reviewed curriculum intended for homeschoolers. Sometimes the school district will offer you their math books free for use as a homeschooler. That is great if you are certified to teach that particular grade level of high school math. You don't want to use a curriculum that assumes you have a thorough understanding of differential equations if you don't even know what they are. A homeschool curriculum will not assume that a math major is teaching in a classroom. Instead, it will assume that a parent like you is teaching a child like yours. When you choose a curriculum intended for homeschoolers, it will hold your hand through the process of teaching. That's why choosing a curriculum intended for homeschoolers is much more helpful, and will make you more successful.

Make sure the curriculum has a video tutorial. Many children need an explanation and some examples. When my children were working on Algebra 1 and Geometry classes, I had no problem providing this tutorial myself. During our morning meeting each day, I would go over how well they did on their lesson the previous day. After a while, it became too much for me. Video tutorials can be very important so your child can see and experience examples before they have to do it on their own. You can also look for a curriculum that has online or telephone help available - somewhere you can call to get any additional resources or answers you need.

It is nice to think that curriculum manufacturers are perfect and their answer keys are perfect. However, I have never seen a math curriculum with every single answer in the answer key correct, not even at the college level. Occasionally, you'll find an incorrect answer. Almost every curriculum will have a couple of incorrect answers in the answer key. This is where online or phone help can be useful. If the answer your child gets doesn't match the answer key and they're confident they got it right, most of the curriculum manufacturers will have any corrections available online. If they have online or phone help, you can contact them for help.

One of the problems I ran into was that every time my children got an answer wrong, they were 100% confident their answer was the right one and the answer key was wrong. I told my children that if they felt the answer key was wrong, they could call the toll-free number or contact online help to find out the correct answer. I would be happy to give them credit for that answer if the help line agreed with it, but otherwise it was marked in agreement with the answer key, as incorrect.

Chapter 3

Correct Attitude

They say attitude is everything and I believe this is especially true for studying math. Try not to instill a fear of math. Do what you can to make it as tolerable or enjoyable as possible.

Don't label yourself a math hater. Don't assume your child will be terrible at math just because you are. Assume confidence and ability – tell them it just takes practice and they'll be able to get it in time. I call this the "fake it 'til you make it" strategy of math.

Pretend that math has always been awesome for you. Try to convey a matter of fact attitude rather than a sense of horror. It's okay to feel overwhelmed, but you want to convey a sense of confidence, strength, and calmness that your children will get it.

Occasionally, a parent has never taken Algebra 1 and it can be scary when their child is in Geometry or Algebra 2 class. You can explain in a calm, confident manner by just saying why you weren't able to get past Algebra 1. Perhaps you were in public school and couldn't keep up with the quick pace of lessons. One of the joys of homeschooling is that you can always make sure your children are confident, even if you weren't.

Invest in your weaknesses. If you feel math is your weak area, work on it first. Put math first in your priority list; it's the first subject you ensure gets done each morning. Don't assign it with a sense of punishment; just explain that it needs to be done quickly and go on to other subjects from there. Make it the first thing you do in the morning and make sure you get it done. It is the number one priority in terms of your time. Even if something fabulous comes your way, or somebody hands you Super

Bowl tickets for your family of eight, don't go to the Super Bowl until math is done. If you know it's your weak area, it's your priority, no matter what comes up.

Investing in your weaknesses also means investing your money. If math is your weak area, then spend the most time choosing your math curriculum. Be willing to spend the most money on it. If your curriculum isn't working, you are allowed to purchase additional curriculum in your weak area, even if you're already one or two months into the school year.

If math seems overwhelming and you find that you never get around to doing it, just remember that every homeschool parent has at least one subject they feel insecure about. For me, it was fine art; I never got around to doing fine art in our homeschool, which is easier to compensate for than math. If you're not getting around to doing it, identify that subject as your weak area and make sure you get to it every single day.

Chapter 4

Correct Speed

The correct speed to cover the material is the speed that's right for your child's level. Teach math at their level and continue moving forward. Keep that forward momentum, for every level of math. Complete one lesson every day and strive never to miss a day.

Most parents know that children can lose some math skills over the summer. In public school, it will often take three months of review each fall to catch up again. It can help to do a bit of review over the summer months, especially for math-reluctant children. Otherwise, it can be easy for kids to forget what they learned. Working on math over the summer can speed things up!

When you review math over the summer, just give three to five problems a day. Nothing horrendous, bulky, or inconvenient, just a bit so they keep those synapses firing and can maintain what they learned over the past year. When they start working on full lessons in the fall, they won't have lost much of what they learned.

It's not a mistake to teach your child eighth grade math if they're in twelfth grade. That is how God made them and you're just being obedient by teaching them at their level. It's also not a mistake to teach your child Algebra 1 in seventh grade if they're ready for Algebra 1 – this is the right level for them.

The first three chapters in a math curriculum are often a review of the previous year. It is okay to skip a lesson if they already know the content; skip the lesson and move on. If you sense your child already knows the material in the first chapter, give them the end of chapter test on the first day of school.

You can bribe them by promising to skip the whole first chapter and start on chapter 2 if they get 80% on the first test. They can be done earlier in the year. It can also do a lot for your child's self-esteem. Even if you personally feel like you're a math failure, this is a great way to compensate for that with your children. It can be a real encouragement for them, even for the reluctant kids, to skip a chapter.

Homeschool moms tend to expect perfection. In math, it's very important to expect mastery but not perfection. Like you, I have mastery over addition, subtraction, multiplication, and division, but I make mistakes from time to time. Consider your own checkbook for a moment. I regularly make math mistakes in my checkbook! At homeschool conventions, I have been known to calculate sales tax on a book five or six times before I know it's right! I do have mastery, but not perfection. My guess is you don't, either. Let's think about this in terms of cooking; when I cook, I have mastery over cooking and can cook for large crowds. When I cook for my family, they're always pleased. I can put on a Thanksgiving dinner like nobody's business, but I am not perfect. I can mess up when cooking by dumping a cup of olive oil on homemade sweet potato fries instead of just a drizzle. And no one in my family will ever forget when I made my famous lemon bars and forgot ... wait for it ... the lemon!

If you have a perfectionist in your family, which is often the firstborn child, be very careful to teach them that there's a very big difference between mastery and perfection. When you make a mistake in your own cooking, your own checkbook, or while writing, just say, "Oops! I made a mistake." It's a clear example of the difference between mastery and perfection. If you are waiting for perfection before moving on, it will be frustrating to everyone in the long run.

Only God is perfect. Yet for some reason, we expect our children to be perfect at their schoolwork and at math. That's not the goal – the goal is mastery. Don't try to achieve the impossible "perfection" in math.

You also want to consider what counts as reasonable compliance. It would be awesome if your children were always 100% engaged in their lessons, but life's not like that. Your goal isn't for your child to sing the praises of math all day long or be successful and perfect at everything. You're just trying to get them to be reasonably compliant.

It's like any work. Everybody has jobs to do; some of those jobs are pleasant and others aren't. When you change your baby's diaper, you don't have to be singing the praises of the dirty diaper. You don't have to love it; you just have to do it. Your child just needs to be reasonably successful in math, and understand it reasonably well.

Four years of math is required. For some, that means a daily struggle over four years that will end in Algebra 1 at the end of high school. It's not optimal, but it does happen. For other kids, four years of math can leave Mom or Dad in the dust as the child pushes forward into Calculus class and beyond.

Chapter 5

Curriculum Options

The best math curriculum to choose for your homeschool has more to do with fit than anything else. When choosing a high school math curriculum, it should have very little to do with the parents' personal preference. It should have a lot to do with your children's personal preferences. You will often not know the important, unspoken preferences your teenager may have.

One girl told me that she hated her math video tutorial because the man in the video looked creepy. As the parent, you might never have thought the man looked creepy; this was her personal preference and could be an impediment towards her learning. Give your child the option of checking out the video first.

Some kids don't like blackboards and some hate whiteboards. A very sociable child may need to see a face to learn best. Teenagers will have a personal preference that may not be the same as yours. The only way you can choose the right curriculum for them is to have them view the video tutorial in advance so they can choose to learn in a way that makes sense for them.

Here are just a few of the most popular math programs available.

Saxon

The most common homeschool math curriculum is definitely *Saxon*. It's top-rated by most math experts. I asked my nephew, who is a public high school calculus teacher, what curriculum he likes. He said that *Saxon* is by far the best and he wished he had the freedom to use it in his school.

In our homeschool, I forbade my children from using *Saxon* at first. I thought it was the most boring math curriculum I had ever seen. I didn't care how highly rated it was or how convenient it was to purchase. We started to fail at math after a while and I needed help. My son opened up the *Saxon* math book and said he wanted it. He explained that it didn't have a bunch of distracting pictures, just numbers. That had never occurred to me; I thought children would want pictures of people happily doing math. Having nothing but numbers seemed boring to me. You can see how personal preference can come into play. You, as the parent, might think that *Saxon* looks less than ideal, but if your child likes it, then it's going to work best for them.

Currently, *Saxon* has three video tutorials available that work with the program. Make sure you look at all three of the video tutorials that complement the *Saxon* program so you can choose the one that's the best fit for your child.

Dive into Math videos are the original ones designed for use with *Saxon* books and are intended for Christian homeschoolers.

Saxon Teacher videos are created by Saxon and go through every problem in the text, including tests.

Homeschool with Saxon videos feature a live instructor, and are intended for a wide variety of classroom and homeschool settings, so they may have a bit of a classroom feel.

Teaching Textbooks

The next curriculum I see used most often is *Teaching Textbooks*. Created by Harvard graduates, it offers video lessons and demonstrations of every problem in the workbook. The newest version is self-grading and lets parents delete lessons for children to do over. This can be handy if your child sometimes gets lazy with math, or completely misunderstands a lesson. Some homeschoolers believe there aren't enough practice problems, but others find it just right. As with any other curriculum, it's about choosing what fits your child.

VideoText

You might consider *VideoText*, an interactive, video-based curriculum that has been around for many years. Even decades ago, homeschoolers that I know were able to pop in their *VideoText* VHS and were successful with that program.

Chalkdust

Chalkdust is another curriculum that has been around forever. This DVD program was especially popular in years past.

Thinkwell

Thinkwell is a more recent addition and it's very well liked. I have heard some of my Gold Care Club members complain that it only allows the child to take a test once. That can make it very difficult if your child doesn't do well and you want them to repeat a test.

ALEKS

ALEKS is a very popular math program. It's a video-aided instruction program for independent learners. However, it's web-based and has no textbook. That can be frustrating if your child gets distracted at the computer, or if you try to limit how many online programs your child does.

Math-U-See

Math-U-See is also a very popular option, especially for children that struggle with math. Homeschoolers tell me it's very good for hands-on learners. Many of the concepts it teaches are math games I used with my children when they were young.

Ask Dr. Callahan

Ask Dr. Callahan is a video series that works well with Harold Jacobs' *Algebra* and *Geometry* books. We loved the Harold Jacobs' *Geometry* and Harold Jacobs' *Algebra* in our homeschool. I was able to teach them Algebra 1 and Geometry using these books because that was all I remembered from high school. Now *Ask Dr. Callahan* has video tutorials that complement these books.

Life of Fred

Life of Fred is a fairly new and unique curriculum. It is a literature-based curriculum that has children read stories about math to explain math concepts. If you have a literature-loving child or one who just loves to read, *Life of Fred* might be worth looking into. In the past, I was hesitant to recommend it because there weren't enough practice problems. *Life of Fred* now have additional practice problems available through their website. Make sure your child gets enough practice to do well on the SAT or ACT. Having math explained in a way that makes sense to your child is invaluable and worth every penny.

A Beka and Bob Jones

A Beka and *Bob Jones* are high school math programs that are both set in a classroom, school environment. If your child once attended school and you have withdrawn them, then a curriculum that imitates school may not work for them. I would not recommend *A Beka* or *Bob Jones* if your child has been withdrawn from school, or has failed math in a classroom setting. It would not likely be a good fit.

If you want to read reviews of different math programs, I suggest you look at Cathy Duffy's book, *102 Top Picks for Homeschool Curriculum*. As you read reviews of the different kinds of curriculum, remember that the one that fits your child is going to be best for them. It might not necessarily be the highest rated curriculum, but it will still be best for your unique child. If your child does not fit *Saxon* and only learns a little because it doesn't make sense to them, they're probably not going to score well on tests. But if they use a lower rated curriculum instead and it makes sense to them, they're going to learn more and score better on tests.

Chapter 6

Games and Supplements

There are many ways to make math fun. Teach your children that math is fun when they're in elementary school and middle school using the many great games and books available. If you have young children, check out the www.LivingMath.net website for a math-based literature book list. There are fun read alouds and even some titles for the upper grades. This is an especially great way to supplement math if you have an avid reader on your hands.

When your child gets more advanced, check out the book, *Algebra the Easy Way*, which is in story form. The author is a man I know quite well, Dr. Douglas Downing, my son's economics mentor. He teaches at the university my children attended. It's a great, fun story that can help kids who love literature get engaged in math.

We also used *Family Math* books quite extensively. The main *Family Math* book is designed for Kindergarten through eighth grade. *Family Math for Middle School* is for seventh through ninth grade. Each book costs about $20-$25 on Amazon and they are filled with math games you can put together easily at home using everyday household items. *Family Math* books would make an especially good investment if you live overseas or are a military or missionary family. Most of the games are multi-age so the whole family can play together. Your math reluctant older child can be encouraged to teach these math games to their younger siblings. At the same time, they can firm up the concepts in their own mind. Teenagers could start a math group for younger kids, maybe even the ones they already babysit. Teaching is the best way to learn and your child will become more confident in math by teaching little ones.

At the high school level, our favorite hands-on activity was *Patty Paper Geometry*. This is a series of creative experiments involving cutting, pasting, and drawing. They teach circumference and other geometry concepts, one-step at a time. My children sometimes found them a little too easy because geometry came naturally. Geometry did not come easily to me, though. As I taught my children using this, I kept thinking it was genius and wished my teacher had taught me with it. I loved it and I'm sorry my children didn't love it; I strongly recommend it, especially if your child doesn't have a good grasp of geometry.

A class called Calculus Made Clear, from *The Great Courses*, was the favorite part of math for my two kids. It's a video lecture on calculus. It simply discusses calculus concepts. We watched it three times: at the start of Pre-Calculus, towards the end of Pre-Calculus, and at the beginning of Calculus class. My children even picked it up and watched two more times just for fun because they found it so interesting.

Another fun supplement is the Khan Academy website, which offers free online classes. Lessons teach specific concepts needed to learn about side angles, side theorems, and geometry, for instance. Look up specific concepts and access the tutorial.

If your child needs more practice, or more work on a certain math concept, consider one of the *Keys to ...* workbooks on the topic. There is a whole workbook just on fractions, as well as a variety of books on other concepts.

On the other end of the spectrum, there are kids that race through calculus; it's easy for them, they like it, and they may want to be an engineer. They might even finish studying calculus by the time they're sixteen years old and you just don't know what to do next. Look into MIT Open Courseware classes. These college-level classes are offered through the Massachusetts Institute of

Technology. Your child can take these free classes beyond Calculus class by using open courseware from MIT and other colleges.

This can be a little overwhelming and I just want to say that I understand how you feel. There came a point when I didn't know anything in math anymore. When my children learned calculus, I didn't understand any of it. I failed Calculus class in college the first time, until my husband-to-be tutored me. Even then, I still didn't understand what I was doing and merely manipulated numbers without understanding what it all meant. When my children took Calculus class, I was so far in over my head – it wasn't even funny. I didn't recognize what the symbols meant. If I saw the answer in the answer key, I couldn't even read the answer aloud because I didn't know how to say the words based on the symbols used.

Here's what "teaching" Calculus class looked like. First, I gave my children the video tutorial. Then they would work through the lesson on their own. If they were stuck, obviously they couldn't turn to me, so I would give them the answer key. They could look back and forth at the solution manual and their answers and work their way through.

Once a week, we would come to the test. At that point, I took the solution manual away with me while I went to the grocery store and let them take the test. When they finished, they would hand it to me. I would open up the answer key and their answer had to look exactly the way it looked in the answer key. It didn't matter if my children claimed their answer meant the same thing; the answer had to be formatted exactly the same way.

There were times when my children were "sure" the answer key was wrong and they were correct. I gave them the option of calling the 800 number or contacting the publisher to find out if the answer key was wrong. As much as they protested, I think they only contacted the manufacturer three times.

If your child needs more math practice, you might want to try using SAT and ACT guides. Check out *11 Practice Tests for the SAT and PSAT* and *Cracking the ACT with 3 Practice Tests*.

Chapter 7

Nine Ways to Actually Get Math Done This Year

When you get into the upper grades of math, it can seem to take FOREVER to get a math lesson done. In fact, sometimes it can be so overwhelming it's even tempting to skip math from time to time, and then you find yourself WAY behind in the book. Has that ever happened to you? Homeschoolers want to get math done each day, but they can't seem to get it all done in the year. Here are nine steps that can help.

1. Teach Short Lessons

It's not a coincidence that public high schools typically have 50-minute classes. Scientific studies have shown that it's difficult to sit and pay attention to one subject for more than 50 minutes. That's one of the reasons why the Charlotte Mason approach works so well; shorter lessons are the best way to maximize learning. To be more successful in your homeschool, consider breaking up your lessons into smaller study periods. Alternate the more intellectual math lessons with something more physical, whether that's P.E., art, music, or any other subject that makes children get up and move around.

In the earlier grades, it's not uncommon to get math done in 30-50 minutes. When you get into upper math levels, it's much more difficult to finish a whole lesson in that 50-minute time period. I taught my children to work on their math for an hour, get up and do something else, then come back to it later in the evening. I have stubborn children though, and I wasn't always successful in getting them to get up and get moving. I noticed that their work slowed down after 50 minutes. It's like the theory of diminishing marginal returns, the more time it takes after the 50 minutes, the slower the progress. It starts to feel like it's never going to end – it may take three hours instead of half that. Your child can get math done more quickly if they stop at the 50-minute mark and come back to it later.

2. Put Weak Areas First

If you have trouble getting a math level completed in a school year, chances are it's not one of yours or your child's favorite subjects. When you've identified something as your weak area, make sure it is the first subject worked on each day. Have your child get up, get dressed, eat breakfast, and then work on math for no more than 50 minutes. Later in the day, they can return to finish up the lesson if needed. Because it's your priority, that lesson has to be completed before you leave home for the day, no matter what. Even if you get hold of free Super Bowl tickets, nothing comes between you and your child and math.

Because it's your weak area, it's also the area you give yourself permission to purchase a new curriculum if your current one just isn't working out. Of course you can't do that for every subject, but it's okay for math because it's your weak area and you will get your money's worth out of it.

3. Have a Morning Meeting

Each morning, have a meeting with your child to go over their daily lessons. If you have many children, you may not think it possible, but you only have to have a short meeting with each one. You can also group grade levels together if you need to, or even space them out every other day.

The purpose of the morning meeting is to check in with your child. Tell your child about an upcoming test, make sure you set up their video tutorial, check their lessons, and check up on how they're doing in general. It gives your child a sense that their mom is watching; their parents care that the child is getting things done. The morning meeting conveys an attitude of prioritizing homeschool work.

I will occasionally talk to homeschool moms who found out their child has forgotten to do math for a month or two and they just didn't know. The morning meeting can help prevent this from happening. If you check in with a morning meeting each day, your child may be able to fake it a couple of times, but you're going to figure it out more quickly. The morning meeting can prevent disaster and especially help get that math curriculum complete in one school year. It can help with many subjects – try it, you'll like it!

4. Reward Good Performance

Homeschool moms like to get their dollar's-worth out of a textbook by doing every single problem; I was like that, too! Take a step back, and focus on learning. Is completing one entire lesson in one day the goal? No! Learning is the goal. Don't let all those problems, and concern for the almighty buck, stand in the way of finishing one math level each year.

You can reward your child's good performance with fewer assigned problems. You see, textbook manufacturers can only guess at how many problems your child will need to complete to understand the concepts. Your child may not need to complete them all! I suggest assigning alternating problems first – all odds or all evens - and then correcting their work. If they get almost all of the answers right (80% or better) they probably don't need to complete any more problems. You can reward them by saying, "That's it! No more!" This approach can give children the number of problems they need, but not so many that they feel overwhelmed. It can also help them be a bit more careful because, in theory, they will be more motivated to do a good job and get the right answer. If they don't get at least 80% correct, tell your children in a matter-of-fact way that they need a bit more practice so you want them to work on the other half of the problems later in the day.

Are you still worried about skipping some of the work? *Saxon* says every problem in the book MUST be completed for the complete math experience. Yet, if you look at the back of the *Saxon* book, it provides the answers to alternating problems. That's how schools use the books; they have kids either do odds OR evens for each lesson. You can do that, too, if it works best for your child.

It's important to remember the bigger goal. Our goal is NOT for our children to do every problem in the book. Our goal is for our children to learn. If they're learning, then your job is done for the day and you can reward good performance with less work.

5. Choose a Curriculum Carefully

Choose a curriculum that fits your child. If what you have is working, keep with it! But if it's not working, consider making a change. In the early years, parents often choose a curriculum that's easy for them to teach and use, and that's great! But in high school, it becomes less and less about the parents, and more and more about the preferences of the child.

Allow the student to choose a curriculum that fits them well. That means showing them the video tutorial for each curriculum, and having them choose the one that works the best for them. If the curriculum is missing a concept or two, any gaps can be filled when they start working on SAT or ACT preparation.

6. Avoid Over-Supplementing

When a math level doesn't get done in a year, it can be tempting to think your child just isn't getting it, when often it's simply a matter of priorities and organization. So if you think, or know, that your child just isn't getting it, avoid over-supplementing to the point where you are working for hours a day on the most-hated subject they wish to avoid. That can truly cause some burnout for everyone in the family and teach your child to hate math! If your child doesn't like math, make sure you serve it up in reasonable bites of math each day. Make sure they do a whole lesson each day as long as that's humanly possible. It's tempting to supplement, add, review, and re-review concepts. Don't double up with more than one math curriculum. Here is what I suggest; if they just aren't getting it, it's probably a curriculum mismatch. Choose a different curriculum.

However, once your child reaches the high school years, keep in mind that it can take two hours to complete a lesson. If your child gets into Calculus class, it can even take up to three hours a day to get a lesson done.

7. Expect Mastery, Not Perfection

I think I have mastery over addition, subtraction, multiplication, and division. But I promise you, I'm not perfect, even with those basic arithmetic skills.

Remember, nobody is perfect. Don't expect perfection in math, or your child will never finish a math level. Instead, ensure mastery of the concepts. Maybe that means they get 80% on tests before moving on, but that's OK. Perfection is an unattainable goal; mastery is attainable and it's what you're trying to achieve in your homeschool. Keep math challenging but not so overwhelming that your children hate it.

8. Adjust Your Expectations

Make sure your child completes one level of math every year in high school. State requirements, college requirements, and employers will all want to see math every year of high school. However, colleges and states do not usually require a calculus credit, so adjust your expectations.

Teach your children at their level in math each year. That's how they will continue to learn and be more successful on the SAT or ACT. Pushing them too hard, too fast, can make those test scores worse. They won't understand the concepts if math is overwhelming. If they're failing Algebra 2, don't continue right into Pre-Calculus because they'll just get farther behind. That's one of the reasons public schools have terrible graduation rates, because they just keep going, even when the kids don't understand. One reason homeschooling works is because we can make sure that our child understands before moving on to the next level.

Sometimes we expect our children to be at grade level and assume that just because our child is at a certain age or in a certain grade they should be in a certain level of math. Not everybody needs to learn calculus by graduation, and not everybody needs to learn algebra in seventh grade. The most common time to start algebra is eighth or ninth grade. It's not uncommon for a child in public school to start algebra in tenth grade.

Make sure your child works on math every year, even in senior year, even if they already have four math credits. Colleges want to see math taken during senior year. College orientation will often include taking a spontaneous standardized math test, to place incoming freshmen in the correct math class and to see whether they need remedial help. The test can be very challenging if your child didn't take math in senior year.

When possible, keep moving forward with math. If that isn't possible, consider statistics or business math for your senior. Some colleges do require a calculus credit, usually for engineering programs or for entry into Ivy League colleges. Check with colleges your child is considering, just to be sure.

9. Embrace Hard Work

Math is the gateway to college and career success. Upper level math is flat-out hard work. Hard work gives your children a good work ethic, which is something they will use every single day of their lives. The ability to work hard is useful no matter what your child decides to do.

While it's tempting to flippantly say, "When will we ever use this stuff?" The truth is they will use it often. If you learn upper level math, simple daily math challenges you face as an adult become easier. One day, I had to adjust a photo for a blog post and I had to use ratios, proportions, and algebra. You could do it the hard way, and guestimate your way to the proper dimensions, but using algebra saved me time. I also use the same work ethic and problem solving skills I used in math. When I worked as an RN, people could die if my math was incorrect.

How do you get your lazy child to work hard? It comes with practice. My friend's son went from homeschooling high school into the work force and was shocked by the poor work ethic of the people around him. He realized that as much as he had failed at math, he had certainly learned how to work hard.

Check out my handy, printable **Get Math Done Checklist,** here:

http://www.TheHomeScholar.com/pdf/9-Ways-to-Actually-Get-Math-Done.pdf

Chapter 9

Math Records

Math on the Transcript

If your child is gifted and ahead in math, some of those classes taken when they were younger may be included as early high school credits. If your child completed an Algebra 1 or higher class, it goes on their high school transcript even if they took it in seventh or eighth grade, or earlier.

If your child is a bit behind in math, your job is to teach math every single year and honestly convey the math content in your class titles. If you teach mathematics rather than Pre-Algebra in ninth grade, that's what you put on the transcript. If your child completes Pre-

Algebra in eleventh grade, that's what you put on the transcript. Teach math every single year and honestly reflect your child's level in the class titles.

Sometimes homeschoolers skip around the curriculum, then end up not knowing what they covered each year, especially when they have remedial learners. Look at what their ability level is currently. Have they taken Geometry or are they at Algebra 1 level? Then count backwards from there. If they are working on Geometry class this year, then last year they did Algebra 1 because you have to have Algebra 1 in order to work on Geometry. That means the year before must have been Pre- Algebra, and the year before that was likely Mathematics. Count backwards to determine the class titles to use on your child's transcript.

Write Course Descriptions

Write course descriptions for your math courses. It's easy. List what your child did, what you used, and how you graded. "What you did" might include one paragraph describing your homeschool class, for example, "In this class, we will cover the content of a high school Algebra 1 course." "What you used" can be simply the math textbook. If you used supplements, such as math readers, video tutorials, hands-on math games, or a field trip, include them as well. "How you graded" includes the sum total of everything you evaluated.

Don't base the entire grade solely on tests – it's not just about the final exam. In math, perhaps one-third of your grade is your child's daily work, one third is tests and quizzes, and the remaining one-third is projects. You can even give your child extra credit if they used additional workbooks. I have yet to meet a professor or teacher that gives 100% of the grade based on tests. The highest percentage I've ever seen is 50% of the grade coming from tests. I encourage you to find a balance: one part of the grade based on tests, one part on their daily work, and one part on projects or additional workbooks.

Conclusion

The Home Stretch

Don't Be Afraid

While math can be difficult, math does not hurt people. It will not hurt the parents, it will not hurt you as the teacher, and it will not hurt your children. Math itself will not hurt your children, but the fear of math most certainly will.

Fear of math will stand in your child's way. Fear of or frustration with math is like a disease that your children catch from you. I know one adult who was told she was too stupid to learn how to read in fourth grade. She never learned how to read or write very well. It has been an impediment throughout her life because she was labeled incapable.

Give your children confidence instead. Encourage math, especially for your girls. Our society doesn't always value mathematical abilities in girls, but that hard work and brain exercise is good for everyone in all walks of life. If necessary, reward your children with cookies. In our home, we rewarded our children with brownies and called them Brownie Points.

Apply Your Knowledge

Take the information within these pages and apply it to other subjects, especially your weak areas. Check in with your child each day using a morning meeting. Put those weak areas first. Cover the core classes. Math is a core subject – it's hard to do but you have to work on it every single day, just like other core classes.

Reap the Rewards

Math is important because your children can reap the rewards no matter what their college or career goals. It can help build a healthy work ethic and problem-solving skills.

Math is also important for earning scholarships. Math classes can help you exceed expectations. If your child is good at math and they do get to Calculus class in high school, they've exceeded expectations. Not everybody has Calculus under their belt; it's fairly unusual. If your child completes the normal amount of math, then math can improve their test scores. If they get a good SAT or ACT test score, they can earn better scholarships.

Let's face it, math won't be a career choice for everyone. It is, however, a very important skill for daily living. I have often watched the news and prayed that God would raise up a generation of leaders who understand – in a profoundly meaningful way – that a trillion dollars is a whole boatload of money! Every time a plane crashes, a bridge falls, or a patient dies because of a hospital error, you can bet that someone, somewhere messed up the math. We all wish that would never happen, but it does. Let's make it our goal to stem the tide of math mediocrity!

Math is important and, for some children at least, it will be fun. Studies show that adult attitudes about math have a profound effect on whether children grow up to be math lovers, math haters, or just indifferent about math. It turns out that moaning about math isn't such a good idea. Kids are wonderful mimics, so let's all try to give them a positive perspective on math. You can help make the world a better (and safer) place!

Appendix 1

The HomeScholar Answers Parent Questions

In this section, I answer questions that have been asked by real homeschool parents on the topic of high school math.

Question: What math levels should my daughter complete in order to be prepared for the SAT?

Answer: Most of the questions on the PSAT/SAT/ACT are about mathematical understanding. Having a good understanding of math is going to help more than if she gets into Calculus class and is way over her head.

The bulk of the questions on those tests involve Pre-Algebra, Algebra 1, and Geometry. If you have completed those three levels before junior year, then you have the chance of scoring quite high on those tests. If possible, try to get that information into them before junior year. If that's not possible, remember that the SAT and ACT tests are taken at the end of junior year. Even if you just fit in Geometry in junior year, then they should have more information by the end of the year.

Question: How do you make difficult questions simple, and the 'Why" and 'How' of doing equations?

Answer: That's what comes mostly from video tutorials and making sure the curriculum is a good fit for your child. If they can't explain those difficult questions in a simple way for your child, then that is not the curriculum for you.

If you run into difficulty with a problem or don't understand the "how and why," then read that tiny section of the book and look for some key words. Maybe the key word is side-angle-side, percentage, or associative property. Look up that key word by going to the Khan Academy website.

If it's in Algebra 1 or earlier, look in the *Family Math* book and find a math game for those concepts. That's how I used the *Family Math* book in the elementary and middle school years myself. I would look up the concept in Kevin's math book and look in the index to find a math game using that concept. On the same day, we would play that math game for 15 minutes. I would pick on Alex the next day, look at his math book and choose the keywords on his math lesson for that day. The *Family Math* book is a multi-age curriculum; it's meant for K – 8th grades so both of the kids could do those games that we played which were extremely effective.

If you're still having trouble with the questions that seemed difficult, then it's probably a curriculum mismatch. When you don't understand something as important as math, then that is the right time to invest the dollars to re-purchase your curriculum.

If you're flailing around in math and do that for years, your child isn't going to score very well when the time comes for the SAT test. If you purchase another $100 curriculum and your child scores better on the SAT test, it might mean a $5,000 scholarship. That $100 math program could get you a $5,000 scholarship or a fabulous job all of a sudden. When it's your weak area, especially when it's math, it will pay off to re-purchase a curriculum when necessary.

Question: Should I grade the work or should my child do it?

Answer: We alternated grading. Correcting their day-to-day work didn't last very long and certainly not by the time they got into junior high; they would correct their day-to-day work. When it came to tests, they were something I would correct.

When we were at high school level and if it didn't look exactly the way the answer key said, I had no way of knowing whether their answer was right or wrong. It had to look exactly like the answer key or I just wasn't able to give them a correct answer.

Question: Is upper math needed?

Answer: Four years of math is needed. Again, it's that good work ethic you're trying to teach your children. You want them to learn how to work hard so they can work hard in the real world.

Having four years of math is important, because as adults, you do lose a part of the math you used to know. If you can get as far as possible into math, then at least you still have something left when you lose the last three years of what you learned. For example, I did get into Calculus and lost all of Calculus, all of Pre-Calculus, and at least half of Algebra 2. But I still retained Algebra 1 and Geometry in my head.

Upper math is necessary to get into college, but a specific level of math is not necessary. You can find colleges that don't require Calculus or Pre-Calculus classes. I know an adult who got into college with only Pre-Algebra, but he didn't graduate from college because he couldn't achieve Algebra 1 in college so it wasn't optimal for him.

Upper math can be necessary for your child's career goals. It's not uncommon to see families with a child who wants to be a computer programmer. It's very difficult to get into college for computer programming unless you have Calculus class, so you do need to work hard at that. I've also known children that wanted a job so bad that they graduated homeschool high school with just Algebra 1 and took three years in a community college until they could get their math up to the correct level. Math is necessary and colleges do like math; they will reward you financially.

Question: What do you do when both you and your student don't understand the materials?

Answer: When that happens, you know that you likely have a curriculum mismatch. When you switch curriculum, it's important to recognize that you haven't understood what was going on before. Make sure to give your child a placement test when you switch curriculum.

For example, if your child used *Teaching Textbooks* and they're not doing well or did horribly on the SAT or ACT test and you know that you have to make a change, don't just pop them into the next level of *Saxon*. Give a placement test so that you know and you'll find out if you have a gap and that you need to go back and do Geometry all over again.

If you find yourself in this situation, look at video tutorials and choose one that makes sense to you and your child. Look at the Algebra 1 videos so you're looking at something familiar to use and look at it together. Once you've decided, then you give them a placement test so you know where to start.

Question: My children took Pre-Calculus last year but we're having difficulty moving on to Calculus. We used *Teaching Textbooks* so what do I do next?

Answer: I've heard from some homeschoolers who have used *Teaching Textbooks* and find it does well to a certain point and then it's very difficult to make the transition into higher math areas. I suggest that you look at other curriculum, perhaps *Saxon*. Give them a placement test to see whether they need to repeat Pre-Calculus before going on to Calculus.

I can't stress enough how important that *Calculus Made Clear* video is – we got so much use out of it. When I think about my own experience with Calculus and how I had no idea what I was doing, I was just manipulating numbers and retained nothing from it; it would have been nice to know what I was doing and I personally could have used that video tutorial when I was in college taking Calculus class.

In *Saxon* math, the step after Algebra 2 is a book called *Advanced Math*. It's a very confusing book for many homeschoolers. The *Advanced Math* book is not intended to be completed in one year; it is one year of Pre-Calculus plus a half a year of Geometry mixed up together like it's been in a blender.

If you haven't taken Geometry, *Saxon Advanced Math* can take a year and a half. If you already took Geometry, then completing it in one year shouldn't be difficult because you can skip the lessons that have to do with formal Geometry and just use the rest of the book. Otherwise, it's hard to get through.

A lot of being successful depends on your understanding of geometry. There may be a few concepts in geometry they're missing that can be easily filled. Some of the curriculum will let you identify any gaps that you have. It will say, "If you miss this problem, here's the concept that you don't understand and here's the page where we explain that concept." For some kids, you'll identify just the specific concepts they're missing.

Question: Is there a downside to *The Great Courses*?

Answer: *The Great Courses* tend to be very expensive. They price them high and then discount them like crazy;

sometimes it'll be 80% off randomly throughout the year. If you don't get a good price, such as less than $100, then look for it at your public library. Sometimes your public library can even order it for you so that you can use it for your homeschool a couple of times during the year.

Question: How do you motivate an unmotivated math student?

Answer: Sometimes it can be as easy as choosing the right curriculum. If their curriculum isn't making sense, look first at whether you have the right fit. My own son chose *Saxon*, which is not something I would have chosen; I thought *Saxon* was the ickiest-looking curriculum on the planet and he thought that it was God's gift to warthogs. He loved it and he thrived because it was his choice, so have them look at the video tutorial first.

Sometimes you just run into an unmotivated student and it has nothing to do with math; it has to do with being unmotivated in general. I do have an article about lack of motivation in teens on my website, which might be helpful. Sometimes it means that something is getting in the way - technology or video games, for instance - and they can't concentrate on math problems.

Other times, it can be their hormones getting in the way. Sometimes boys need to be almost to the point of physical exhaustion in order to concentrate on something like math. Their hormones just make it hard to concentrate on anything. It's one of the reasons we were very involved in sports with our children; they were involved in swim team and soccer team. Other homeschool parents I've talked to have made sure their children are near exhaustion by having them play basketball first and then come in to do their math work. Or they might have a paper route and then do their math work, something to help them to sit down and settle down.

You can also experiment by putting math first each day. Sometimes kids just aren't bright until after lunch. Maybe you can put something else first in the morning, but math is something that you can put first thing after lunch. They've been outside and they've played outside, and then they can settle down and it's okay because it's after lunch. Experiment with the time when they can be most capable of sitting down and focusing. Then there is always bribery using food – that's what we did.

If your child does have some gaps or needs extra practice worksheets, a lot of that can come from practicing with SAT or ACT prep. That will pick up any missing pieces that might need some practice.

Appendix 2

Homeschooling Geeks

Homeschooling geeks - what a challenge! Somehow, we need to make it work. We are called to be the best home educators we can be for our beloved nerds. If you have a geek or nerd on your hands, other parents are likely jealous of your child's math ability or at what a whiz they are with computers. They are amazed you can successfully teach math or computer science at home. If only they knew you were just hanging on by a thread! Together we can figure out how to get this job done. Parents of geeks and nerds, unite!

When you think about it, now is a great time to be a geek or nerd. They can find like-minded people on TV shows and movies dedicated to geeks and nerds. The four pillars of geekiness are STEM: Science, Technology, Engineering and Math. These core competencies are hot topics, as most people today believe they are vital fields for the future. Often these interests will earn big scholarships and financially lucrative careers.

Don't you wish there was a user's manual for these kids? They can be as difficult to decipher as a Java manual written in Mandarin! Let me make it simple for you. First, understand that geeks will be both awesome and annoying, so accept both. Second, do as much as you can to feed the beast and fuel those passions in your children. Third, watch for warning signs that could indicate trouble finding a balance in their love for technology. Fourth, be ready to collect the credits they accumulate naturally.

Awesome and Annoying

Teaching geeks can be awe-inspiring as we watch them love and learn advanced subjects and technology that we can't even dream of understanding. They seem to learn beyond limits and absorb information the way we absorb the sun's rays on a summer day. I've spent many days reading "fluff" literature while my child was knee-deep in nerdiness. If you're not a geek or nerd yourself, you have to wonder how they do it. How can they learn such remarkably boring stuff? It's not boring to them. For some geeky reason only they understand, they love it!

But geekiness has a downside. It can be incredibly annoying. The sounds they make as they chatter away with their tech talk, and the discussions they have (or try to have) with others can be frustrating for parents. They can far-surpass our understanding of technology or other topics, leaving us mere mortals feeling incompetent and inept. But take heart! Annoyance can often mean real learning has taken place, and high school credit can be granted. Even though you feel like you are in over your head, you aren't supposed to be "teaching" at this level anyway. They are supposed to be learning independently, so it's not necessary for you to understand them. This is where the rubber meets the road - where they begin to take their own path.

Feed the Beast

Tech-loving geeks can be like starving teenagers. It's a challenge to feed the beast and keep them satisfied! Provide the curriculum they need. Try to find hands-on experiences with like-minded geeks. Locate clubs, groups, fairs, and competitions that will interest your child. Techie teens can enter competitions, and enjoy the experience and a chance to interact with others who have similar interests. Competitions like these look great on a homeschool high school transcript. They can be listed on their activity list, demonstrating social skills and passion. Leading a group in their interest will indicate leadership skills. Using their skills on the job can earn money for college.

For tech-lovers, check out *First Lego League* and the *Lego Robotics League*.

Look into the *USA Computing Olympiad*, *Science Olympiad*, and other local science fairs and math competitions. If your child earns a certificate for ham radio or Java, include it on their transcript. At some point, you will need to go beyond the basics in science, technology, engineering or math. If your child is ready to go beyond high school basics in technical subjects, don't shy away, dive right in! There are plenty of resources online. Check out Khan Academy for high school level courses. If your child is ready for college level classes, you can look into Coursera.org or MIT OpenCourseWare. Don't worry - you don't need to know the material or even teach it!

Find opportunities for your child to learn on their own. Geeks and nerds will enjoy learning across the curriculum with their passions. The topic that is their obsession can even be incorporated into subjects such as English, history, and art. Have them read and study books on the topic, write essays or stories, look for historical parallels, and create works of art or a short film. Give them credit towards each subject their work touches on!

Watch for Warnings

Beware of missing subjects. Plan early for college prep classes, because your child is more likely to want or require a college degree. Your geeks and nerds are going to need to cover all the bases required to enter college. They need to cover the major branches of science, not just the one they like most, studying biology, chemistry, and physics. Computer geeks will need Calculus class as well. In general, the more science and math they get in high school, the better, because they'll need it for an engineering or computer science degree. At the same time, don't double up on classes by making them take a class in something when they already know the subject.

Cover all the core classes. To get into a STEM program, kids can't study STEM subjects exclusively; they will need the other core classes. Include English, reading and writing, every year. They may enjoy reading classic literature that includes titles in the fantasy or sci-fi genre. Consider these books to add to your child's reading list: *Alas Babylon, War of the Worlds, Brave New World, The Lord of the Rings,* and *A Wrinkle in Time*. Cover the fine arts, too, perhaps in a geek-friendly way, with a subject like digital photography. Make sure you complete a foreign language. They may enjoy Latin because it's more logical than other languages, so check to see if that is an acceptable language to colleges you are considering. Be sure to include PE, so you can demonstrate a well-rounded individual.

Watch out for the pitfalls of technology. Computer geeks do a lot of their work in various digital formats. Because being a geek or nerd tends to involve excessive computer use, make sure you and your child are both familiar with the signs and symptoms of internet addiction. Set reasonable boundaries, and teach your child the importance of monitoring their own computer use. You can find a collection of helpful articles on my Pinterest Internet Addiction Resources board. Discuss the appropriate use of technology together with your teen and set logical boundaries with the help of my article, "TechnoLogic: Setting Logical Boundaries on Technology with Your Teen," found on my website, www.TheHomeScholar.com

Collect Credits

Allow natural learning. If your child is learning math without you (don't laugh – it can happen!) you don't need to teach it again. Give your child a placement test in math to determine their math level. Fill in any math gaps with SAT Prep Books such as *The Princeton Review's Practice Tests for the SAT*. These prep books can be used as math "worksheets" to cover any missing links. This way you will fill gaps and study for the SAT at the same time, so it's a win-win situation. They are especially useful for kids who have excelled in math and need a review in basic concepts in order to score well on the test and get into the geeky college of their choice.

Encourage delight directed learning. Use their geeky or nerdy pursuits for high quality electives. Your child may be learning computer languages or other highly technical skills that are typically studied in community college or university. If your child demonstrates mastery in a technical subject, give them credit on their high school transcript. For example, if they are fluent in C++, you might give one credit with the class title, "Computer Programming: C++." If your child is participating in robotics competitions, you can award one credit and call it "Robotics" or "Introduction to Robotic Engineering." If your child is an intern, use that experience as their Occupational Education credit. This is another class your child can include on the transcript every year (some classes may repeat every year).

Collect college credits when you can. Sometimes learning goes beyond the normal high school subjects. While there are a few AP and CLEP tests in technical categories, more techie subjects can be found in DSST tests. These tests make wonderful outside documentation for highly technical skills and your child can get two for the price of one, high school credit AND college credit through one test! Just remember to check if the colleges your child is considering award college credit for these tests.

Describe each class with detailed course descriptions. Since geeks can do some crazy stuff, just writing "Technology" for the class title isn't enough. Describe exactly what your child did, learned, or experienced. Make a list of what they used and provide some indication of how you graded - just remember that you do not need to include tests in your grading criteria, because there are plenty of other ways to evaluate learning.

Free Math and Programming Resources

Your average child may get to Pre-Calculus or Calculus in high school using standard homeschool curriculum, but your geek may need much more math in order to feed the beast. There are free resources available for upper level math.

Don't forget that library resources are always free. Ask your librarian about AP Calculus resources you can use. Find *The Great Courses* course called "Calculus Made Clear" to provide a clear explanation of calculus concepts while encouraging a love for upper level math. Here are some free resources for math experts. Some are completely free or available for a free trial period. One of these resources may be just the encouragement your little Einstein needs right now!

- *Khan Academy: Calculus*
- *Brightstorm Math*
- *TheMathPage.com*
- *Lamar University Math Tutorials*
- *ExploreLearning.com: Interactive Math*
- *QuickMath: Automatic Math Solutions*
- *SOSMath: Calculus*
- *SOSMath: CyberExam Practice Tests*
- *COW Math: Calculus on the Web*
- *MidnightTutor*

There are free resources available for computer programming. You don't need to buy an expensive coding curriculum if your child is interested in programming computers. Here are some great free resources for techies to try:

- *Codecademy.com*
- *Khan Academy: Computer Programming*
- *Coder Dojo*
- *Learning Code the Hard Way*
- *Eloquent Javascript*
- *The Code Player.com*
- *HTML5 Rocks*
- *Developer Mozilla: Learn How to Make Websites*
- *Google Developers University*
- *UDACITY.com*

Error 404: College not Found

As you are guiding your geek, remember that the path to techie happiness often runs through college first. Even a child who is happy being on the Geek Squad now may later decide to become a computer engineer. Always be prepared for career shifts and make sure your child is prepared for college admission and scholarships. A love of all things techie is not enough to get into engineering school. They need the whole package - even math and the fluffy, artsy, human-based subjects. Educate yourself about college preparation with my book, *The HomeScholar Guide to College Admission and Scholarships,* which you can find on my Amazon author page: www. amazon.com/author/leebinz

Here is the bottom line: relax! Let your computer geek or math nerd learn what they can without you. Along with the usual homeschool classes, give them what they crave. Provide the opportunity and resources to pursue their own, delight directed learning, while you enjoy scooping up credits for their homeschool high school transcript.

Afterword

Who is Lee Binz and What Can She Do for Me?

Number one best-selling homeschool author, Lee Binz is The HomeScholar. Her mission is "helping parents homeschool high school." Lee and her husband Matt homeschooled their two boys, Kevin and Alex, from elementary through high school.

Upon graduation, both boys received four-year, full tuition scholarships from their first choice university. This enables Lee to pursue her dream job - helping parents homeschool their children through high school.

On The HomeScholar website, you will find great products for creating homeschool transcripts and comprehensive records to help you amaze and impress colleges.

Find out why Andrew Pudewa, Director of the Institute for Excellence in Writing says, "Lee Binz knows how to navigate this often confusing and frustrating labyrinth better than anyone."

You can find Lee online at:

www.TheHomeScholar.com

If this book has been helpful, could you please take a minute to write us a quick review on Amazon?

Thank you!

Testimonials

Practical Help and Encouragement

"I was a member of your Gold Care Club and my daughter was immediately accepted to universities and offered their highest merit scholarships. I never could have achieved this without YOUR initial research! I don't think I would ever have considered private schools until I met you and heard how feasible it really is. Thanks for holding my hand through the first few years when I had anxiety over the thought of a FAFSA or application essay! It's no longer a mystery, just a lot of hard work."

~ Rebecca

"Lee's Materials are a GIFT"

"Lee, you are AWESOME. My two daughters are at a University, with financial aid and an academic scholarship that I fully credit to your *Setting the Records Straight* book and other transcript making materials! I tell EVERYONE who asks, "I just did exactly what Lee said to do!" Lee's materials are a GIFT! The University LOVED her transcript and was HAPPY to accept her and gave her an academic scholarship, on top of her FAFSA grants. She is majoring in Engineering and LOVES college! We are so grateful for all of your materials! Thank you, LEE!"

~ Dana

For more information about Lee's products, go to:

http://www.thehomescholar.com/parent-training.php

Also From The HomeScholar...

- The HomeScholar Guide to College Admission and Scholarships: Homeschool Secrets to Getting Ready, Getting In and Getting Paid (Book and Kindle Book)
- Setting the Records Straight - How to Craft Homeschool Transcripts and Course Descriptions for College Admission and Scholarships (Book and Kindle Book)
- Total Transcript Solution (Online Training, Tools and Templates)
- Comprehensive Record Solution (Online Training, Tools and Templates)

- Gold Care Club (Comprehensive Online Support and Training)
- Preparing to Homeschool High School (DVD)
- Finding a College (DVD)
- The Easy Truth About Homeschool Transcripts (Kindle Book)
- Parent Training A la Carte (Online Training)
- Homeschool "Convention at Home" Kit (Book, DVDs and Audios)

The HomeScholar Coffee Break Books Released or Coming Soon on Kindle and Paperback:

- Delight Directed Learning: Guiding Your Homeschooler Toward Passionate Learning
- Creating Transcripts for Your Unique Child: Help Your Homeschool Graduate Stand Out from the Crowd
- Beyond Academics: Preparation for College and for Life
- Planning High School Courses: Charting the Course Toward High School Graduation
- Graduate Your Homeschooler in Style: Make Your Homeschool Graduation Memorable

- Keys to High School Success: Get Your Homeschool High School Started Right!
- Getting the Most Out of Your Homeschool This Summer: Learning just for the Fun of it!
- Finding a College: A Homeschooler's Guide to Finding a Perfect Fit
- College Scholarships for High School Credit: Learn and Earn With This Two-for-One Strategy!
- College Admission Policies Demystified: Understanding Homeschool Requirements for Getting In
- A Higher Calling: Homeschooling High School for Harried Husbands (by Matt Binz, Mr. HomeScholar)
- Gifted Education Strategies for Every Child: Homeschool Secrets for Success
- College Application Essays: A Primer for Parents
- Creating Homeschool Balance: Find Harmony Between Type A and Type Zzz...
- Homeschooling the Holidays: Sanity Saving Strategies and Gift Giving Ideas
- Your Goals this Year: A Year by Year Guide to Homeschooling High School

- Making the Grades: A Grouch-Free Guide to Homeschool Grading
- High School Testing: Knowledge That Saves Money
- Getting the BIG Scholarships: Learn Expert Secrets for Winning College Cash!
- Easy English for Simple Homeschooling: How to Teach, Assess and Document High School English
- Scheduling - The Secret to Homeschool Sanity: Plan You Way Back to Mental Health
- Junior Year is the Key to High School Success: How to Unlock the Gate to Graduation and Beyond
- Upper Echelon Education: How to Gain Admission to Elite Universities
- How to Homeschool College: Save Time, Reduce Stress and Eliminate Debt
- Homeschool Curriculum That's Effective and Fun: Avoid the Crummy Curriculum Hall of Shame!
- Comprehensive Homeschool Records: Put Your Best Foot Forward to Win College Admission and Scholarships
- Options After High School: Steps to Success for College or Career

- How to Homeschool 9th and 10th Grade: Simple Steps for Starting Strong!
- Senior Year Step-by-Step: Simple Instructions for Busy Homeschool Parents

Would you like to be notified when we offer the next *Coffee Break Books* for FREE during our Kindle promotion days? If so, leave your name and email at the link below and we will send you a reminder.

http://www.TheHomeScholar.com/freekindlebook.php

Visit my Amazon Author Page!

amazon.com/author/leebinz

Made in the USA
Middletown, DE
25 March 2018